Little Leaders

Backyard Adventure

Learning About Colors
with Casey Camel, Tibo Tiger & JoJo Giraffe

written by Bradley Silvius

It was a beautiful,
sunny day outside.
Tibo swung on the swing,
and JoJo slid down the slide.

Tibo was about to ask JoJo for a push
when he saw something move
behind a bush.

With flowers like roses, tulips, and a daisy...

What was it? An animal? Or a bird?

For a minute, Tibo thought his

vision might be a little bit hazy.

Then it moved again.

Wait, that's a hat...

and out stepped Casey!

Casey, what are you doing

on this beautiful day?

Hi, Tibo and JoJo!
Want to visit my
back yard and play?

What a great idea,
since Casey had a pool.
On such a hot day,
they could stay cool.

Casey, your hat is so colorful and bright. It reminds us to be thankful for our sense of sight.

Remember the story
of Joseph and his brothers.
Joseph's Dad gave him a
coat of many colors.

"Yes," said Casey.

"That story does come to mind.

And here in the back yard

are many colors we can find."

I'll go first
and start way up high.
If you look above,
you'll see a **blue** sky.

"That's awesome, Casey!
Look what I found,"
as Tibo pointed at the
green grass on the ground.

The other day, we had rain showers.

Now we can enjoy these **purple** flowers.

The garden is also a very colorful place

with **yellow** corn,

red tomatoes,

and an **orange** pumpkin
with a smiley face!

Red, **Blue**, and **Yellow**
are called Primary Colors.

They blend together
to make all the others.

I have paint, brushes and paper here.

Let's mix and see what other colors appear.

Red mixed with **Blue** makes **Purple**!

Red mixed with Yellow makes Orange!

Yellow mixed with **Blue** makes **Green**!

Joseph was thankful for the colorful coat from his Dad. Casey, we are grateful for the fun that we've had.

Thanks for inviting us
to play in your yard.
We will show our gratitude
by sending you a card.

Little Leaders®
LITTLE TODAY. LEADERS TOMORROW.®

Tibo and JoJo headed home
as the sun went down,
happy to have learned about
the colors they had found
and appreciation for
God's creation all around.

Hey, Friends! Now that we have seen so many beautiful colors, let's have some fun coloring these pages!

See if you can choose the right
color for the object on each page.
It will be so much FUN!

What color is a fire truck?

What color is the ocean and sky?

What color are the bananas?

What color is the grass?

What color is the pumpkin?

What color are the grapes?

Did you know?

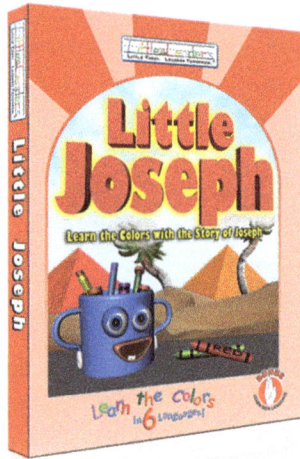

This book makes a great companion to the **Little Joseph** episodes of The Little Leaders Video Series!

Ready for more Backyard Adventures?

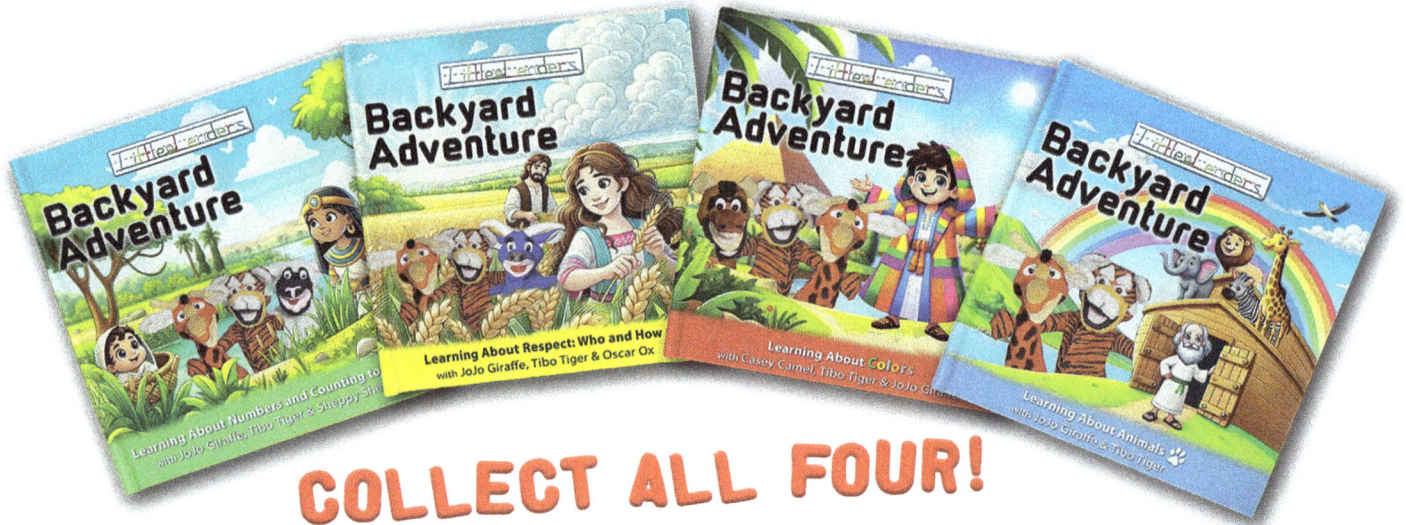

www.ingramcontent.com/pod-product-compliance
Lightning Source LLC
Chambersburg PA
CBHW040248100426
42811CB00011B/1196

* 9 7 8 0 9 7 5 9 8 0 2 2 4 *